Original title:
My Life: A Comedy of Errors

Copyright © 2025 Creative Arts Management OÜ
All rights reserved.

Author: Nora Sinclair
ISBN HARDBACK: 978-1-80566-028-6
ISBN PAPERBACK: 978-1-80566-323-2

The Joy in Missed Connections

I missed the bus, I missed the train,
Chasing shadows, driving me insane.
With every twist, a new delight,
Laughing at my clumsiness tonight.

The coffee spilled, the toast was burnt,
A small mishap, a lesson learned.
I tripped and fell right on my face,
Yet found a smile in every place.

Laughing Through the Chaos

A jumbled mess, but oh so dear,
I wear my fails like jewels to wear.
Slipped on a banana, oh that was grand,
Left my dignity in the medic's hand.

Lost my keys and found a shoe,
Wandered off, not sure what to do.
Yet in the frenzy, there's a song,
These silly gaffes, they never last long.

Chasing Mistakes in the Moonlight

Under stars, where dreams collide,
I danced with blunders, my trusty guide.
The night was ripe with silly whims,
I twirled with laughter, sang my hymns.

Starlit paths led me astray,
Each wrong turn, a new ballet.
In every fumble, joy does bloom,
Lighting up the darkest room.

My Eloquent Errors

Words that stumble, thoughts that slide,
In every blunder, I take stride.
A slip of tongue, a laugh so bright,
My eloquence, a comic sight.

I wrote a letter, mailed it wrong,
To my pet goldfish, where I belong.
Yet in this chaos, I hear a cheer,
For every error brings me near.

The Circus of Mistakes

In the ring of blunders bright,
Clowns tumble left and right.
Juggling tasks that slip and slide,
Laughter follows like a guide.

A trapeze of plans swings high,
Landing softly with a sigh.
Every turn a new delight,
In this circus, wrong feels right.

When Plans Go Awry

Maps in hand, I take a stride,
Turn the corner, lost inside.
Each step's a twist, a funny flop,
Up is down, and round we hop.

Coffee spills upon my shirt,
As I dodge a lurking dirt.
With each stumble, giggles grow,
It's the best show, don't you know?

Joy in the Jumble

Life's a puzzle, pieces stray,
Finding fun along the way.
When the socks refuse to match,
Laughter is the perfect catch.

Dinner burns, the smoke alarm,
Yet in chaos, there's a charm.
We dance through each silly slip,
Savoring every little trip.

The Comedy of Misfortune

Stumbling through each opened door,
Tripping over plans galore.
Falling up the stairs in glee,
Oh, the joy of being me!

With a wink and playful grin,
Life's mishaps are how we win.
Each misstep leads to the laugh,
Embracing all, we've found our path.

The Jester's Missteps

In bright attire, I prance with glee,
But trip on laces, oh, woe is me!
The crowd erupts in a roaring cheer,
For laughter is found in my small sneer.

A pie in the face, oh what a sight!
Giggling children, my pure delight.
I juggle dreams, but they slip away,
A jester's fate on this silly day.

A Tumble Through Time

With time on my side, I spin and sway,
Yet slip on banana peel - oh, what a day!
Past and future swirl in a messy dance,
Who knew mischief had this much romance?

Clocks tick and tock, they create the fun,
As I fumble and bumble, I know I'm not done.
Stumbling through moments, with giggles abound,
In this circus of life, joy's always found.

Laughter in the Wrong Places

In a quiet cafe, I spill my drink,
Laughter erupts, no time to think.
A slip on the floor, the world spins around,
With clumsy grace, I fall to the ground.

Strangers chuckle, their faces aglow,
As I tell a joke that was far from pro.
Every misstep, a punchline divine,
In the most awkward moments, I truly shine.

The Clown's Misadventures

Red nose and big shoes, I set out to play,
But trip on my tail - it's a classic cliché!
With each silly stumble, I spread joy like rain,
For laughter can lighten the heaviest pain.

A crow on my shoulder, a cat on my feet,
This circus of chaos is quite the feat.
In every blunder, I find my own spark,
For the heart of a clown lights up the dark.

Chronicles of a Clumsy Heart

Tripped over my own two feet,
Tumbled down, what a sight!
Laughter echoed in the street,
As I regained my balance, bright.

Coffee spilled upon my shoes,
How did I become the clown?
All my plans, I must refuse,
For chaos wears a lovely gown.

I texted wrong, sent hearts to friend,
She thought they were for her instead.
Joyful mischief never seems to end,
Life's a script with lines misread.

Yet in these blunders, I find glee,
Adventures spark in each mistake.
Embracing quirks, I dance with me,
In this waltz, I choose to shake.

The Paradox of Perfection

Chasing dreams with running shoes,
Every step, I trip and fall.
Perfect plans lead to confusion,
Who knew I'd hit the wall?

Juggling tasks, I drop them all,
In my rush, I lose the game.
Striving hard, I heed the call,
Yet mischief is my middle name.

Mirror, mirror, looks deceive,
Perfect hair? A hairpin fails.
All my efforts, I believe,
Are tangled up in funny tales.

With no precision, here I stand,
Laughter's echo in my wake.
Embracing flaws, the world's my brand,
In this comedy, I partake.

Wit in the Whirlwind

In a whirlwind of pure chaos,
I twirl around and around.
With a grin, I feel no loss,
For humor is my solid ground.

Stumbled words make awkward laughs,
Each joke lands with a twist.
Life's a stage, and like its halves,
I find joy where I can't resist.

Countless slips, and yet I thrive,
A circus act in every jest.
In the mess, I feel alive,
With every joke, I'm truly blessed.

So when the storm begins to howl,
And troubles dance a merry jig,
I'll grin and wave, wear the scowl,
This jesting heart will always dig.

Fumbling Towards Freedom

Steps uncertain, I sway and bend,
Dancing through life's bizarre parade.
With every tumble, I ascend,
In laughter's light, I'm unafraid.

Every plan I try to make,
Turns into a comedic show.
Mistakes befriend, they never break,
They paint my world with vibrant glow.

Hiccups in my grand design,
Like comic strips, each moment thrives.
In messy lines, I brightly shine,
Living fully, that's how I strive.

So here's to blunders, one and all,
Each misstep leads to joy anew.
Fumbling towards freedom, hear the call,
In quirky messes, I find my cue.

The Quirks of Quixotic Questing

I set out to find a treasure,
But tripped over my own shoe.
The map was a dazzling pleasure,
Yet led me to the nearest zoo.

With lions that laughed at my plight,
And monkeys that swung from the trees,
I pondered my curious fight,
And forgot all my grand guarantees.

The compass spun wild with glee,
Pointing right when I went left.
I ventured to scale a tree,
But ended up quite inept.

In a quest that went off the rails,
I discovered what truly shines:
A laugh at the smallest fails,
Is worth far more than gold mines.

Hiccups and Humor

Hiccups burst forth with a bang,
Each one a surprise to my throat.
Unexpectedly loud, they sang,
While I tried to remain afloat.

Around friends, it turned to a game,
With challenges shared through a laugh.
I hiccuped right out of my name,
And we all lost our balance, half.

A hiccup, a snort, a quick dance,
Fumbling like I had two left feet.
In mishaps, I found a fine chance,
To turn stumbles into a treat.

With every small spurt and jest,
Life's quirks are a sweet little scheme,
Each hiccup's a humorous fest,
A giggle, a giggle, a dream!

Laughing at the Looming Lament

When plans fall apart at the seams,
  And worries hover like clouds,
I find a way to turn to dreams,
  And chuckle, despite the crowds.

With socks that never seem to pair,
  And coffee spills on my shirt,
I stand in the whirlwind with flair,
  Proclaiming, 'This is absurd!'

Life's little pitfalls bring joy,
  A slip on a banana peel,
Turns frowns to flamboyant coy,
  As laughter becomes our appeal.

With each turn of fate's cruel wheel,
  Humor breaks down every wall,
In every blunder, we reveal,
  That laughing is the greatest call.

A Dance of Dubious Decisions

I signed up for a dance class,
Expecting grace, poise, and flair.
But tripped on the light in the glass,
And landed in quite the scare.

The instructor raised an eyebrow,
As I spun and then quickly fell.
Yet with every awkward bow,
I rolled with laughter, quite well.

My feet led me down paths unwise,
With steps that could only confuse,
But in the madness, I saw the prize,
As my friends and I shared the blues.

We twirled in a crazy charade,
With falls that are legends today,
In every euphoria displayed,
Humor dances in its own way.

Blunders Beneath the Stars

Under blinking stars, I trip and fall,
Stumbling on shoes that just don't fit at all.
Laughter erupts from the shadows nearby,
As I chase my dreams, I stumble and sigh.

A dance with a broom, I sweep the whole room,
While juggling my hopes, I create such a gloom.
My cat watches close, with a flick of her tail,
As I conquer this chaos, I almost prevail.

But the pizza delivery guy shows up late,
With soggy old boxes, now that's my fate!
I laugh at the mess, the blunders I make,
In the moonlight, I twirl, for fun's not at stake.

Under the vastness, each gaffe's a delight,
A symphony of errors, all wrapped up tight.
I wink at the stars while I dance through the night,
For joy comes from laughter, igniting my flight.

Smiles Amidst the Scrutiny

In a crowd's keen gaze, I spill my drink,
A splash of soda makes everyone think.
With a sheepish grin, I wipe it away,
While my friends burst in laughter, come what may.

A fashion faux pas with mismatched socks,
I strut down the street, feeling like a fox.
Strangers raise brows; I see them all stare,
But I just throw a wink and flip back my hair.

A meeting gone wild with ideas so bright,
I mix up my words, a comical sight.
A proposal for cats instead of a plan,
The boss shakes his head, but I'm still the fan!

Through scrutiny's lens, I wear joy like a crown,
With smiles in the chaos, I never back down.
In this circus of life, I revel in glee,
Finding laughter within all the mishaps I see.

Giggle-Fueled Gratitude

Mornings bring mayhem, toast stuck in the slot,
A breakfast disaster, but I'll give it a shot.
Butter goes flying, colliding with walls,
Echoing giggles, oh how laughter calls!

The dog chases squirrels, ignoring the leash,
He bolts like a rocket, it's chaos unleashed.
Neighbors just chuckle, they know the routine,
In this goofy drama, I can't help but beam.

In moments of blender disasters in sight,
Smoothies explode, oh what a delight!
I dance in the mess, joy bubbles outside,
Each moment a treasure, I cannot hide.

With every small blunder, I raise up a cheer,
In this giggle-fueled life, there's nothing to fear.
I savor the blips, the blunders, the fun,
For in every mishap, my heart's always won.

Unfolding the Unforeseen

With plans in my pocket, I set out today,
But the bus goes the wrong way; where will I stray?
I wave to the driver, and he waves me back,
The world spins in circles, what else could I lack?

A detour through laughter, I find my own path,
Dodging small puddles, avoiding the wrath.
A stumble on curbs leads to giggly spills,
In this unpredictable trip, my heart surely thrills.

I twist to the left when I mean to go right,
Each twist and each turn is a comic delight.
The surprises unfold, like a playful prank,
As I navigate life with a cheerful heartfelt thank.

In the tapestry woven with blunders and fate,
I see the joy bloom, I celebrate late.
With a chuckle and grin, I embrace the unknown,
In this whimsical dance, I've always been shown.

The Art of Fumbling

I tripped on my shoelace, what a sight,
The pavement greeted me, oh so tight.
I laughed at myself, how absurd,
Life's little slips, not so unheard.

Each coffee spill is a new surprise,
As I mop it up, I realize.
The world is a stage, I'm the clown,
In this grand act, I never frown.

My phone takes a dive, into the stew,
Like a fish out of water, what's a guy to do?
With a shrug and a grin, I'll carry on,
In this dizzy dance, I'm never gone.

So here's to the blunders, the twists and turns,
In every fumble, a lesson learns.
With a wink and a smile, I'll make it shine,
For every mistake is a punchline divine.

Joyride on a Cracked Road

A flat tire made me laugh and sigh,
As I waved to strangers, wondering why.
The GPS led me quite astray,
But I found a café at the end of the day.

With each wrong turn, I saw new sights,
A quirky shop or weird fight nights.
A detour becomes a fun escapade,
With snacks and laughter, I'm not dismayed.

The road is bumpy, but who's to care?
I spread my arms, let down my hair.
Wind in my face, giggles in the air,
Life's cracked road turns into flair.

So here's to journeys, wobbly and wild,
Every misstep, a happy child.
In the backseat of chaos, I'll reside,
With a joyful heart, I take the ride.

Punchlines and Pitfalls

I slipped on a peel, oh what a fall,
The laughter erupted, I gave my all.
With a flourish I bowed, to my adoring fans,
In this circus of slips, nobody plans.

A sneeze in a meeting, a loud "Achoo!"
The silence that followed, what can you do?
With red cheeks and giggles, I take the stage,
In this book of blunders, I'm turning the page.

A dog stole my lunch, right out of hand,
I chased him around, but he took a stand.
With a bark and a wag, he made quite a show,
In the play of mistakes, I'm learning to flow.

So grab life's punchlines, don't take a fall,
In the grand comedy, we're all standing tall.
With laughter as glue, we stick through the night,
In a world full of blunders, we find our delight.

The Laughter Between Mistakes

In a world of mishaps, I find my way,
With each little trip, I seize the day.
The coffee I spilled, now a running joke,
In the echoes of laughter, I never choke.

With every misstep, I dance a bit more,
Life's funny rhythm, hard to ignore.
The falls and the stumbles paint smiles anew,
In the laughter between, joy breaks through.

Sweet awkward moments, they fill up the air,
As I trip on my words, I just don't care.
With friends by my side, we laugh till we cry,
In this grand act of living, we'll keep flying high.

So let's raise a toast, to all that we find,
In the humor of gaffes, we'll never be blind.
For life is a series of giggles and grins,
In the laughter between, our joy always wins.

Quirks and Quakes of Daily Life

I tripped on my shoelace, oh what a sight,
The dog gave a bark, took off in mid-flight.
Coffee spills down, like a canvas of brown,
I wear my mishaps like a glittery crown.

The toast pops up, flies straight to the floor,
The cat gives a glance, then walks out the door.
With socks that don't match, I step out for a stroll,
My outfit's a riddle, a comedic goal.

In grocery lines, I count all my change,
My pocket's a circus, it's feeling so strange.
Forgotten my list, I'm lost in the aisle,
The fruits all start laughing, and I join the smile.

But each little blunder, I take with a grin,
Life's just a game, and I'm here for the win.
So bring on the quirks, let's dance through the mess,
In this comic ballet, I couldn't care less.

A Palette of Peculiarities

With paints that run wild and colors so bright,
I splatter my canvas, oh what a sight!
The brush slips away, just a swish and a swirl,
And I end up with art that makes heads all twirl.

In a pie-eating contest, I dare to partake,
Only to realize, I'm pie and I shake.
Each bite is a challenge, a frothy delight,
As visions of berries dance through the night.

I plant all my seeds, in the wrong earthy bed,
Now carrots grow tall, and the tomatoes look red.
The plants have conspired, they've plotted their tricks,
I'm the jesting gardener caught up in their mix.

Each moment's a stroke, a laugh on the page,
In this quirky mosaic, I embrace every stage.
So let's paint with abandon, no rules in our way,
For life's absurd canvas is where I shall stay.

Awkwardness as Art

I waved to a stranger, but turned out it's Joe,
He blinked in confusion, and then we both froze.
A dance of mishaps, a tango of fate,
In the spotlight of blunders, we twirl and we skate.

Coffee shop lines get my nerves in a twist,
With a fumble and drop, that croissant's now missed.
I chuckle and sigh, as I stand in despair,
While the barista just grins at my pastry affair.

A text meant for you, went to someone else,
Awkwardness blooms like a springtime of gels.
We laugh about feelings and tales of misread,
Creating new stories, from moments we've bred.

So here's to the awkward, the cringe, and the falls,
In this gallery of life where each blunder enthralls.
The art of the awkward, my favorite charade,
In this comedic journey, my heart won't evade.

Whimsical Misfires

I set out to bake, with a recipe grand,
But flour's my friend, and it just won't stand.
A sprinkle of sugar? Oh where did it go?
The whisk took a holiday, just to steal the show.

I wore my best shoes, a gamble today,
But puddles of rain thought to brighten my play.
Now dancing through droplets, I leap with a cheer,
The circus of life's misfires, oh dear!

A phone on the fritz, it dials in the night,
Poking mischief, it gives me a fright.
My friends all get texts, from my cat's favorite meme,
They laughter rings out, like I'm part of the dream.

So I'll stroll through the quirks, with laughter divine,
Embracing the chaos, the mix-up, the shine.
For life's whims are a dance, a step here, a fall,
A circus of moments, I cherish them all.

The Joy of Jumbled Journeys

I set out bright and clear, the map in hand,
But turns I took, oh misfortune grand.
With every step, a chuckle arises,
In tangled paths, life offers surprises.

The coffee spill, an early start,
As I jogged, my shoes played part.
A dog chased me down the lane,
With laughter, I danced through the rain.

Lost on routes I thought I knew,
With every wrong turn, new friends grew.
A detour here, a fumble there,
A joyful mess, beyond compare.

Through jumbled journeys, life unfolds,
In silly tales, the heartupholds.
With laughter loud and spirits high,
My journey's charm will never die.

The Antics of Unraveled Plans

I planned a feast for friends galore,
But burned the roast, what a chore!
Instead, we feasted on pizza pies,
With funny stories and happy sighs.

The recipe said, 'Add a pinch!'
But I dumped a cup, oh what a clinch!
Sweet turned sour, we laughed out loud,
In kitchen chaos, joy was found.

A trip to the beach became a quest,
With lost towels and a game of jest.
Sand in the car and sunburned skin,
Yet, in mishaps, true fun began.

Unraveled plans, a merry show,
In soft sunlight, our laughter flows.
With every blunder, memories grow,
Life's flat tires can spark the glow.

A Comedy of Contorted Paths

I chased the sun with maps so bright,
But found the shade, much to my fright.
Paths twisted like pretzels laid,
In every detour, new jokes were made.

The elevator broke, I took the stairs,
With every step, I lost my cares.
An accidental slip on a funky sock,
Rolling down, I became a rock.

At work, misprints flew all around,
My 'urgent memo' became a sound.
The boss just smiled, his gaze sincere,
In blunders shared, camaraderie here.

Through contorted paths, I will roam,
With every laugh, I feel at home.
The joy in chaos, quite the art,
Life's little messes tug at the heart.

When Misfortune Meets Mirth

Oh, the times I slipped on spilled delight,
Falling into laughter, oh what a sight!
Crispy leaves and stumbles, too,
In every moment, the joy just grew.

A rainstorm came, I lost my way,
With puddles jumping, I chose to play.
Umbrella flipped, a goofy dance,
In misfortune's grasp, I took a chance.

Dinner plans gone astray for sure,
I laughed so hard, forgot to be pure.
Chili too spicy, tears in my eyes,
Yet in all this, joy never dies.

When misfortune meets a cheerful glance,
Life's absurdities prompt a dance.
In every blunder, a chance to spark,
With humor bright, we light the dark.

A Symphony of Snafus

Every morning starts with glee,
Brewed my coffee, spilled it free.
The toast jumps, and my cat prances,
In this chaos, life romances.

Lost my keys in the fridge again,
My socks mismatched, like a clown's den.
I trip and tumble through my day,
Yet somehow laugh; it's the only way.

Dinner plans? A dish I burn,
But find a snack, it's my turn.
With jokes and giggles, I will mend,
Each slip and fall becomes a friend.

So raise a glass to all the blunders,
In the laughter, joy still thunders.
As life writes scripts full of quirks,
I dance along, embracing perks.

Comic Relief from the Mundane

Woke up late, what a sight,
Socks on hands, but it feels right.
Stepped outside, forgot my shoes,
Laughed so hard, I had the blues.

A meeting loomed, my brain's a mess,
Wore a tie, but it's a dress!
Laughter erupted, what a team,
In chaos, we find our dream.

Tried to cook, but smoke did rise,
A culinary act, oh what a surprise!
We ordered out, and to my delight,
That pizza pie was just all right.

Life's a stage with bloopers galore,
Each misstep opens another door.
In the circus of everyday play,
I wear my heart, in a funny way.

Laughing at Life's Left Turns

I bought a map, I lost my way,
Took a wrong turn on a sunny day.
Discovered a park, quite bizarre,
Chased a squirrel, my own bizarre star.

At work, I sent a meme too loud,
My boss laughed, oh, I felt proud.
Email blunders, each a delight,
I'll keep on laughing, day and night.

Dinner mishaps, burnt my stew,
My pet goldfish took a view.
Through every twist of fate and jest,
I find the joy, I feel so blessed.

With laughter bouncing off the walls,
I celebrate these mighty falls.
Each turn in life may start with fright,
But end in giggles, pure delight.

Falling Flat with Flair

A dance routine, I hit the floor,
Two steps forward, then I roar.
Tripped on heels, fell with grace,
I rolled around, made it a race.

Shopping list? What a joke!
Bought a cactus, instead of smoke.
In a world of perfect fits,
I'm the king of silly skits.

At the gym, I tried to lift,
Weights flew high, a gift adrift.
The trainer laughed, and so did I,
Sweating bullets, I reached for the sky.

Life's a stage, and laughs unwind,
With every blunder, joy I find.
So let's embrace each epic fail,
In falling flat, I'll always sail.

The Funhouse Mirror of Choices

In mirrors twisted, paths confuse,
I trip on laughter, shout my blues.
Each corner hides a silly fate,
With every turn, I hesitate.

A jester's hat upon my head,
I leap through life, feel light as lead.
Choices echo, bouncing back,
In this vast maze, I lose my track.

With wobbly steps, I dance afar,
In funny shoes, I raise a bar.
The punchline's there in wobbly grace,
I juggle time with a smiling face.

But every stumble brings a giggle,
As I untangle from the wiggle.
Through blunders bright, I find my cheer,
In this grand circus, I persevere.

Jests and Jumbles

Oh what a mess, this life I weave,
With every slip, I laugh, believe.
A pie in face, a pratfall bold,
My stories shared, a treasure trove of gold.

A juggler's trick, a clown's parade,
Through life's ruckus, I'm not dismayed.
In tangled tales and playful jest,
I find my way; I'm quite the guest.

With rubber chickens in my pack,
I march through life, devoid of slack.
Mismatched socks, a comical sight,
Each day begins with silly delight.

At every turn, I'm caught unaware,
Yet laughter bubbles in the air.
These jests and jumbles, my own muse,
In chaotic joy, I can't refuse.

A Witty Wayward Wanderer

A wandering soul without a map,
I wander through each funny gap.
In coffee spills and accidental falls,
I find the joy amidst the walls.

With a twinkle in my eye so bright,
I chase the sun both day and night.
Misplaced keys and altered paths,
Each step I take, the world just laughs.

A witty smile, a clever pun,
Each glance around, I find the fun.
Oh, life's a show, and I'm the star,
With every blunder, I raise the bar.

Through ups and downs, I laugh aloud,
In quirky moments, I feel so proud.
This wayward wanderer, full of glee,
In each misstep, I find the key.

Laughter in the Lapse

In quiet moments, giggles rise,
A slip, a slide, a big surprise.
While timing's off, the punchlines fly,
In every lapse, I almost cry.

A broken vase, a playful cat,
In chaos wrapped, I tip my hat.
The clock ticks backward, time gives chase,
I run in circles, a laughing race.

The hiccup here, the stammered word,
Each blunder dances, laughter stirred.
With jesters prancing through my mind,
A touch of whimsy, joy defined.

In every twist, I find a joke,
With every lapse, my heart bespoke.
Through funny tales and silly cheers,
I craft my life amidst the years.

Playing the Fool with Flair

In a world where plans go wild,
I trip on my shoelaces, yet I smile.
Each stumble brings a chuckle or two,
Life's a stage, and I'm the fool in view.

With mismatched socks, I strut with pride,
Dancing to tunes of a whimsical tide.
A pie in the face, laughter fills the air,
Oh, the joy of playing the joker with flair.

When logic leaves and chaos takes the lead,
I find the humor in every misdeed.
With every mishap, a story unfolds,
My heart's a treasure, worth more than gold.

So let the laughter be my guiding light,
Even in blunders, the world feels bright.
With a wink and a grin, I embrace my fate,
In this dance of woes, I celebrate!

The Palette of Puzzles

Colors clash on this canvas so bright,
Puzzles galore in chaotic delight.
Every mix-up, a splash of fun,
I paint my days 'til the setting sun.

A jigsaw of moments, some pieces won't fit,
Yet in every failure, there's joy with a hit.
The clown's nose bounces, the colors run free,
Finding the humor in what's meant to be.

With brushes of laughter, I color outside,
Each curve and each line, a trusty guide.
In the mess of creation, I find my sweet bliss,
Every awkward stroke is a moment not to miss.

So here's to the palette, so vibrant and strange,
Life's little puzzles, I love how they change.
With giggles and grins, I'll embrace every spin,
For in every misfortune, a new tale begins!

Reveling in the Ridiculous

Oh, what a sight this life can be,
Full of blunders, wild and free.
Punchlines land like clumsy shoes,
In the dance of folly, I simply choose.

With spaghetti on my shirt, I take a bow,
Mistakes become legends, let's savor them now.
Each flop a step in this dizzying race,
Where laughter is gold, and I find my place.

Clowning around, I relish the jest,
In a world of chaos, I find my best.
Slipping on marbles, I break into song,
In the symphony of errors, I feel I belong.

So raise up your glass to the absurd and the fun,
To the face plants and slip-ups, let's toast everyone.
For in reveling madness, our spirits ignite,
With laughter as fuel, we dance through the night!

Twists in the Tapestry

Life weaves a story, with threads so askew,
Twists and turns, yet laughter breaks through.
Every knot ties a tale with cheer,
In the fabric of blunders, I hold them dear.

With a faux pas here and a mishap there,
I stitch up my heart with moments to share.
Each loop and each swirl, a bright shade to see,
In this tapestry knitted, I'm happy to be.

Like an errant yarn, I weave with delight,
Sailing through chaos, it feels just right.
From snags I discover the essence of play,
In every mistake, there's a velvet bouquet.

So here's to the twirls in this colorful seam,
To the dance of the foolish, the joy of the dream!
In this quilt of existence, I'll give it my all,
With humor as my thread, I shall never fall!

Laughing Through the Chaos

In the morning I spilled my brew,
On my shirt, oh what a view!
Matching socks? Not in sight,
I'll wear one black and one bright.

Neighbors watching me from afar,
Chasing ducks, I've lost my car.
Tripped on laughter, oh what fun,
Only to rise, under the sun.

Dinner plans? A jumbled mess,
Burnt the bread, forgot the dress.
Yet we feast on tales so grand,
With laughter's grip, we make our stand.

So here's to blunders, raise a toast,
We'll laugh at what we need the most.
Through hiccups, laughter's the key,
In this wild circus, just let it be.

The Hilarity of Half-Measures

Attempted yoga, lost my way,
Fell on the mat, laughed all day.
With arms flailing, I found my grace,
While the dog joined, what a race!

Tried to cook a five-star meal,
Burnt the rice, but it's surreal.
A quick fix with takeout's cheer,
Pizza delivered—let's all cheer!

A haircut done with far too much flair,
One side short, but who can care?
Hiding the mess with a bold hat,
Oh well, I guess that's where I'm at!

So cheers to plans that go awry,
Half-measures that make us sigh.
Let laughter rise above the fray,
In every stumble, joy finds its way.

Blunders in Bright Colors

Woke up to find my hair a fright,
Yellow streaks, not my best light.
Yet I laughed as I faced the day,
With rainbow hues leading the way!

Fashion choices became a jest,
Stripes with polka dots, I'd guess.
But when I strutted down the street,
Confidence made each mistake sweet.

Dropped my phone and watched it slide,
In a puddle, my woes abide.
Yet a giggle danced on my lips,
As I fished it back with silly quips.

Life's a canvas, wild and bright,
With every blunder, pure delight.
So let the colors clash and swirl,
In the gallery of this crazy world.

Unintentional Playwright

In my kitchen, a scene's set,
A recipe gone, oh what a bet!
With flour flying, it's a play,
A slapstick act—who needs ballet?

The doorbell rings, I trip on the mat,
Landing in groceries, how about that?
With a tumble, I rise with a grin,
And the audience cheers, where to begin?

A mishap dance, an act of grace,
Juggling life in a chaotic space.
For every error, there's laughter's stage,
In this grand play, we turn the page.

So here's to the moments, unscripted and true,
Where comedy thrives in all that we do.
Each stumble a line, a laugh we share,
In the whimsical theater that's everywhere.

The Humor in Helplessness

I tripped on a shoe and fell on my face,
The dog looked at me, a true comedy case.
I laughed at my fortune, while dusting the dirt,
Life's little mishaps can't really hurt.

A taxi I hailed, but it passed me by,
I waved like a madman, with hope in my eye.
The driver just chuckled, he knew he was late,
Yet, here I am grinning, isn't life great?

The toast I prepared, it flew like a bird,
But I had my coffee, so I just laughed and slurred.
The butter was flying, it landed with flair,
These moments of chaos are beyond compare.

With friends, I had planned a grand dinner night,
But we burnt all the dishes, oh what a sight!
We dined on snacks, not quite what we aimed,
Yet laughter and tales left us all unashamed.

Accidental Anecdotes

The doorbell rang, I jumped in surprise,
I slipped on a marbles, what a grand prize!
I fell to the floor, with a laugh and a grin,
These tales of mishaps make it hard to win.

While baking a cake, I mixed salt with the sweet,
I served it to friends, they couldn't compete.
With faces all scrunched, they fought to be kind,
Yet laughter erupted, and joy intertwined.

I wore mismatched socks to an important meet,
The bosses just giggled, my fashion's unique.
I shrugged and I shrugged, what else could I do?
In the world of blunders, I'm the one who's true.

A serious plan turned into a joke,
With umbrellas and rain, I had everyone soaked.
We twirled in the puddles, got lost in the fun,
Accidental anecdotes we spun one by one.

When Plans Go Awry

I set my alarm for an eight o'clock start,
But snoozed it till noon, oh dear, what a art!
With clothes on inside out, I dashed out the door,
When plans go awry, who could ask for more?

The picnic I planned was a total flop,
With ants in the basket, we couldn't stop.
Yet under the sun, we laughed at our plight,
As sandwiches vanished, we cheered at the bite.

A dance I envisioned turned into a spree,
I stumbled and twirled, just my luck, can't you see?
The music kept playing, and I followed the tune,
When plans go astray, the day's still a boon.

As life led me here, I learned to embrace,
The humor in chaos, the trials we chase.
In every misstep, there's joy to unfold,
When plans go awry, our stories are told.

Slapstick Shadows

In a rush to get dressed, I fell from the chair,
Knocking over a lamp, it flew through the air.
It crashed to the ground with a dramatic flair,
Oh how I laughed, life's quirks we must share.

A cart of groceries turned to a display,
I slipped on a banana, what more can I say?
I found myself chuckling while others did stare,
Life's little slapstick can lighten the drear.

The humor in falling, I know it too well,
As I tumble and trip, I just ring my own bell.
With laughter like medicine, we've all got a chance,
To dance through the moments, to slip through the dance.

With friends by my side, we play the fool,
In our slapstick shadows, we rewrite the rule.
We giggle and snort through each foible and mess,
For in every blunder, there's happiness blessed.

Laughter Through the Lens of Life

I tripped on a cat and fell on a pie,
While juggling my thoughts, I let out a sigh.
The world spins around in a dizzy ballet,
Made of slip-ups and blunders that brighten my day.

A squirrel stole my sandwich, oh what a scene,
As I waved my hands like a clumsy marionette queen.
Life throws me curveballs, I laugh at the jest,
Finding joy in the chaos, it's truly the best.

With mismatched socks and a shoe on the wrong foot,
I dance through the hiccups, oh what a hoot!
Every mishap a memory, a tale for the ages,
Written in laughter, my heart turns the pages.

Through lenses of humor, I squint my two eyes,
Each stumble a treasure, each trip a surprise.
In this carnival of moments, I'll twirl and I'll spin,
Collecting my giggles, let the fun begin!

Tales from the Topsy-Turvy

I missed the bus, but the dog stole my hat,
In a world upside down, where it's all about that.
The sky was a puddle, the ground floated high,
   I giggled at clouds that seemed ready to fly.

With shoes on my hands, I pranced in the rain,
   A chorus of laughter, somewhat insane.
A marching band played all the notes out of tune,
  While I spun like a top under a bright afternoon.

My toast burns with pride, as butter takes flight,
   A battle of breakfast, my morning delight.
  Each mishap a story, my life's comic flair,
   In the topsy-turvy, I find joy everywhere.

   As I slip on a smile, I wink at the day,
In this circus of blunders, I'll find my own way.
Every tumble a treasure, each blunder a cheer,
  In tales of the twisted, I hold love quite dear!

Chronicles of Chance Encounters

I bumped into a lamp while searching for my shoe,
It winked at me slyly, as if it knew too.
Streetlights giggle softly, my phone starts to ring,
With the voice of mischief, what a silly thing!

The ice cream truck danced, in a joyous parade,
While cones tumbled down in a sugary cascade.
I chased after flavors, like a bee to its flower,
Every slip and slide, a moment of power.

An umbrella opened, and I flew like a kite,
Through puddles and giggles, oh what a sight!
Chance encounters abound, wrapped up in delight,
Each laugh an adventure that feels just right.

In this book of the quirky, my heart takes a leap,
With stories of laughter tucked safe in my keep.
Life's erratic ways are my favorite muse,
In chronicles of chance, it's joy that I choose!

The Juggling Act of Existence

With breakfast in one hand and phone in the other,
I juggle my worries, and laugh with a smother.
A burst of confetti from a sneeze out of place,
Life's a grand circus in this funny race.

As I trip over socks that have staged a coup,
The cat looks amused, like she knew it too.
I juggle my coffee, my keys, and my dreams,
In this wild performance, or so it seems.

With tasks like balloons that float ever high,
I dance on the edge of a whimsical sky.
Each wobble a giggle, each fumble a cheer,
In this juggling act, I draw laughter near.

Beneath all the chaos, jewels sparkling bright,
I find joy in the madness, my soul takes flight.
In every mishap a reason to beam,
In this show of existence, I embrace the dream!

The Mirth of Mishaps

I tripped on my shoelace, oh what a sight,
Fell into a puddle, soaked and bright.
The cat looked smug, crowned my fall,
As I laughed out loud, what a ball!

Coffee spilled down my brand new shirt,
Thought I was cool, now I feel like dirt.
A dance with fate, a twist of chance,
With all my clumsiness, life's a dance!

The joke's on me, I take a bow,
For every goof, I make a vow.
Life's little blunders, I embrace,
A glorious mess, this wild chase!

So here's to slips and fumbles grand,
With every blunder, I take my stand.
In laughter's warmth, I find delight,
A comedy show, my days ignite!

Joyous Jumbles of Reality

A breakfast flop, the toast flew high,
As marmalade waves waved goodbye.
Eggshells danced atop my plate,
A culinary feat, quite first-rate!

Misread the map, lost in my town,
Asked for directions, got spun around.
Each wrong turn was a laugh, not a fret,
In silly circles, I place my bet.

Wanted to impress with my new moves,
But tripped on the rug, lost my grooves.
The crowd roared, I took a grin,
For in my folly, fun begins!

So bring on the jumbles, the slips and falls,
Each joyful mess, a laughter calls.
Life's a comedy, with quirks galore,
Every blunder opens a door.

The Quirkiness of Everyday Adventures

Mismatched socks upon my feet,
A fashion fail, but oh so neat!
Out the door, I hear a cheer,
"Nice look!" they shout, with high good cheer.

Spilled my drink, what a surprise,
Danced with laughter as it flies.
Each awkward moment paints my day,
In bright colors of a funny play!

Missed my bus, with time to spare,
Joined a busker, gave life some flair.
Sang off-key in the noon day sun,
What started dull turned to such fun!

Embrace the quirks, let worries fade,
For in the laughter, joy is made.
Every blunder shines like a star,
In my comical tale, here we are!

Laugh Lines and Life Lessons

Each wrinkle tells a story, so bright,
Of days filled with laughter and silly plight.
With friends beside me, we forge ahead,
In the theater of life, we're never misled.

Tried to cook dinner, burnt it all,
We opted for pizza—a delicious call!
Cheese and laughter shared with glee,
A delicious mess, just you and me.

Life's little lessons come as a jest,
When everything's crazy, we feel so blessed.
A tumble, a slip, they're just part of the show,
In this comedy, we learn to glow!

So let's toast to the laughs, to the goofy falls,
In every mishap, our spirit enthralls.
With each little trip, oh what a thrill,
Life's punchlines abound; let's laugh 'til we're ill!

A Tapestry of Ticklish Tales

In a world where I trip and fall,
Each blunder's a story, a whimsical call.
I dress in a mismatch, a sight to behold,
Laughter erupts as my humor unfolds.

From spilled drinks to slipping on ice,
Every mistake is a brand new slice.
With a wink and a grin, I take the stage,
Turning each misstep into a comedic page.

Friends gather 'round, they all know the drill,
As I narrate tales that give them a thrill.
With each chuckle, I weave in delight,
Life's circus unfolds, a magnificent sight.

So here's to the errors that make us all smile,
May we stumble through life, error-prone style.
The laughter we share is my greatest success,
A tapestry woven with joy, not distress.

The Delight of Disarray

My coffee's gone cold; what a silly mess,
I wear mismatched socks, feeling quite blessed.
Each morning's a puzzle, chaos at play,
Where laughter and clumsiness rule my day.

I reached for a cookie, but knocked over tea,
A splash and a giggle, oh what a spree!
Dancing with shadows, I trip on the way,
Who knew that my chaos could brighten the gray?

The world seems to chuckle, it joins in the fun,
As I navigate life like a race yet not run.
With friends by my side, we share every fumble,
Creating a symphony out of our stumble.

So here's to the mess; it's perfectly fine,
In the delight of disarray, we all can shine.
With laughter as glue, our lives intertwine,
Each twist is a joy, a reason to dine.

The Comedian's Compass

Lost in the maps of my own creation,
Every wrong turn leads to elation.
A beacon of humor guides my way through,
With jokes as the stars, twinkling anew.

I fumble and trip, but who keeps the score?
Each blunder's an invitation for more.
Like a car with no brakes, I dash down the road,
In the face of mishaps, I lighten the load.

A slip on a banana, oh what a scene,
As laughter erupts, I know what they mean.
The compass I carry points to delight,
In the heart of each moment, I find my light.

So here's to the flat tires and wrongs that I've made,
In the hilarious journey, I'm blissfully swayed.
For within every error lies joy to be found,
And with laughter as guide, my heart does abound.

Stumbling Toward Serendipity

Like a bird with no sense, I flit and I fly,
Finding fortune in folly, oh me, oh my!
Each stumble's a step toward joy unforeseen,
On this quest for the laugh, I'm a comedic machine.

I mixed up the sugar with salt for my tea,
But a sip turned a mishap to sweet jubilee.
With friends in my corner, we roll like the tide,
Every fumble we share amplifies our pride.

In the mess of my days, I discover my bliss,
With each little error, how could I resist?
The dance of the goofy is what I embrace,
In the waltz of mishaps, I find my place.

So here's to the laughter and stumbles I chase,
To the twists and the turns that we all must embrace.
For in laughter's sweet realm, serendipity lies,
Turning chaos to joy, a delightful surprise.

Wobbly Steps and Witty Remarks

I tripped on air and tumbled down,
A laughter track in the bustling town.
With every stumble, a tale to weave,
Where grace and goofiness often conceive.

A coffee spill, a charming charade,
The twist of fate, my grand parade.
I wink at mishaps, dance with fate,
In this circus act, I celebrate.

Socks mismatched, a questionable style,
Each fashion faux pas brings a smile.
I strut and pose, the jokes unfold,
In this absurdity, I'm pure gold.

Life's a jest, in laughter we trust,
With every blunder, there's joy to adjust.
So here's to the missteps we all make,
In this play of life, we're all on break.

Chasing Shadows in Slapstick Style

I chased my shadow, it gave me the slip,
Running in circles, a dizzying trip.
With every misstep, the laughter grew wide,
As I pranced like a fool, with joy as my guide.

Wanted to dance, but I tripped on a cat,
Who stared with surprise, now how about that?
Got tangled in laughter, what a fine catch,
Life's slapstick moments, a skillful match.

A knotted shoelace, a comedy scene,
Fell in a puddle, a splash so serene.
The audience giggled, they clapped and they cheered,
In this wild chase, every surprise appeared.

Chasing shadows, in playful delight,
With each silly blunder, the world's feeling right.
I'll dance through this farce with a wink and a grin,
In this slapstick saga, the fun's just begin.

Sparkles of Sorrowful Humor

Life's little quirks, they glitter and shine,
In moments of sorrow, a joke's on the line.
I wear my heart with a clumsy flair,
Finding giggles in gloom, a breath of fresh air.

In a puddle of tears, I slip and I slide,
With onlookers chuckling, I'm filled with pride.
I stand in the rain, make silly stone faces,
Through the stormy weather, happiness traces.

Each slip on banana peels, life's little jest,
Finding humor where chaos can rest.
With chuckles and giggles, I dance through despair,
In the moments of dark, I embrace the rare.

Bright sparkles of laughter amidst the gray,
In sorrow's embrace, I find a new play.
So let the tears fall—they're just part of the show,
In this theater of life, let the laughter grow.

A Mischief of Moments

A wiggle, a jiggle, a slip on a shoe,
Each awkward moment, a comedy cue.
I stumble through life, with glee in my heart,
Crafting mischief, a spontaneous art.

In the kitchen, a flour storm did arise,
My cake fell down, what a sweet surprise!
With frosting gone rogue, I chuckle and sigh,
This messy endeavor, oh my, oh my!

In the park, I attempt to impress,
Tripped on a bench, oh what a mess!
But laughter erupts, as I rise with flair,
With every mishap, joy's flavor fills the air.

A tapestry woven with humorous glee,
These moments of mischief, they're all part of me.
Each stumble and giggle, a memory bright,
In this playful chaos, I dance through the night.

A Jester's Journey

In clown shoes I roam, a laugh in each step,
Chasing my tail, in mischief I leapt.
With pies flying high, and jokes that fall flat,
Every great blunder's a tale to chat.

At the edge of the stage, I trip on a wire,
A tumble, a roll, my grace to admire.
The audience chuckles, they can't help but cheer,
For folly and laughter are why I am here.

Painted on smiles, I juggle my fate,
With every misstep, I simply can't wait.
To dance with the blunders, to twirl with the jest,
In this circus of life, I'm truly blessed.

So here's to the stumbles, the laughter they bring,
I embrace every pratfall as part of the fling.
With a wink and a grin, I'll take a big bow,
In the theater of chaos, I'm king of the now.

The Art of Tripping Gracefully

With every step forward, I trip on a shoe,
"A masterpiece!" I yell, from my face in the goo.
The audience gasps, then erupts into glee,
A graceful performance, despite my debris.

Pavements are fragile, a dance floor of fate,
I pirouette awkwardly, embrace the plate.
Mistakes are my partners, they lead me amiss,
In this comedy sketch, there's laughter and bliss.

Spilled drinks and misplaced keys, I wear them like crowns,
Oh, the thrill of the stumble, the joy of the frowns.
Life's a grand stage where we all play a part,
And falling with style? That's an art from the heart.

So take off your shoes, let the fun come alive,
In this waltz of mishaps, we truly can thrive.
With humor as armor, we dance through the night,
In the Art of Tripping, we find pure delight.

Punchlines and Potholes

A pothole appears like a trap for my shoe,
I leap and I laugh, oh, what else is new?
Still, I land with a splash, creating a scene,
Like a slapstick routine, I'm the star in between.

With punchlines like raindrops, they fall all around,
I catch them with laughter, as joy does abound.
The world is my stage, with props in the grass,
And every misstep brings a smile that can last.

Chasing the sunset, I trip on my pride,
Yet all of the blunders, they fill me with stride.
Graced by the goofs and the giggles that chase,
In this carnival ride, I'm finding my place.

So say cheers to the errors, the slips, and the falls,
They make life amusing, like punchlines in brawls.
With joy like confetti, I'll dance through the fray,
In puddles of laughter, I'll find my own way.

The Misadventures of Everyday Living

Woke up with my shoes on the wrong feet, how quaint,
Dancing through breakfast, I spill my old paint.
Each morning a mystery, a riddle, a game,
In the circus of life, I'm the star with no fame.

I trip on the carpet, my coffee takes flight,
A swirling tornado of beans in the night.
With giggles and chuckles, I gather the floor,
Every mishap a treasure, who could ask for more?

Grocery aisles hold adventures of their own,
As I reach for the chips and knock over the scone.
Explosions of laughter shimmer in the air,
As I dodge fleeting shoppers, my stories to share.

So let's toast to the blunders, the fun we create,
In this wild tapestry, let's seal our own fate.
With a wink and a grin, let's dance through the day,
In the misadventures, we'll find our own way.

Slip-ups and Surprises

I wore my shoes mismatched today,
Thought it was a fashion sway.
Tripped on air, the world spun round,
Laughter echoed, oh what a sound.

Coffee spilled all over my shirt,
A morning dance, oh what a flirt.
I claimed it was a style so new,
While my boss just rolled her view.

The phone rang, I answered the cat,
Mistook a joke for a real spat.
Friends laughed, falling off their chairs,
I just smiled, forgot my cares.

Life's a sketch, an ongoing play,
Where every stumble leads astray.
We laugh at slips, at choice turns,
For joy and folly, our heart yearns.

Tripping Over Laughter

Walking through life, one foot wrong,
Life's a tune, I can't find the song.
I step on a toe, hear a squeak,
Laughter erupts, so loud, so unique.

With a banana peel, I made my stage,
An audience gathered, trapped like a cage.
"Watch me glide!" I boast with flair,
I'm on the ground, still in the air.

Dinner plans went awry last night,
I burned the pasta, not a delight.
"Crispy!" I yelled, with a broad big grin,
But they all laughed at the mess I'm in.

Every day holds comedic flair,
With every blunder, love is in the air.
So here's to the slips that make us whole,
Life's funny dance, it brightens the soul.

The Farce of Everyday

Socks on dryer, a solo dispute,
Their partner's missing, oh what a hoot.
One leg looks fancy, the other in dread,
Fashion faux pas, but good rumors spread.

I tried to impress with a meal I concocted,
Spices flew wild, my focus distracted.
"What's this explosion?" my friend cried in fright,
"It's a new dish!" I claimed with delight.

A walk in the park, I fell for a branch,
My dignity lost, didn't stand a chance.
The birds just chirped, judgy little crew,
As I laughed it off, with not much to do.

In mishaps I find, the best sort of cheer,
Every blunder brings laughter near.
So let us toast to the silly parade,
For every mistake, a memory made.

Chronicles of a Well-Intended Fool

With every plan, a twist I draft,
Thought I'd be clever, oh what a craft.
Riding high on my ideas grand,
I fell on my face—was it really planned?

I wrote a love note, thought it was sweet,
Sent it to the neighbor, how could I compete?
She laughed so hard, turned bright red too,
Sometimes affection's a comical view.

Lost my keys in the fridge last week,
Fridge full of charm, my brain's at its peak.
As I stood there, I couldn't help but grin,
After all, who else would do this again?

In my story, I'm the jesting sage,
Turning blunders to laughter on stage.
Chasing dreams with a chuckle and glee,
A comical journey, just let it be.

Gags of a Wandering Heart

I set out with glee, a map in my hand,
But turned left instead of right, oh, how unplanned!
The street signs are laughing, I'm late to the show,
Each step I take backward, where on earth did I go?

My shoes are mismatched, a true sight to behold,
While stepping in puddles, I'm feeling quite bold.
The ice cream I bought now drips down my shirt,
Oh, life's little surprises can really hurt!

I tripped over a dog, what a sight I must be,
He gave me a look, like, "Dude, don't blame me!"
The laughter of strangers, like music in air,
In this dazzling disaster, no worries, no care.

So here I meander, the king of lost trails,
Collecting my blunders, like fairy tale tales.
With each silly stumble, a giggle I find,
In the gags of my heart, there's joy intertwined.

Quirks and Quips of Existence

I woke up one morning, hair standing like spikes,
Thought it was a bird, but no, it's just my likes!
With coffee in hand, I tripped on my shoelace,
Spilled half of it right on my sleepy face.

I tried to make toast, but smoke filled the room,
Turns out, my new toaster had the vibe of doom.
With laughter and chaos, it wedged in my heart,
Life's quirky moments, my favorite part!

The cat on the counter was plotting a scheme,
Knocked over my lunch like it's part of a dream.
Yet in the midst of it, with giggles in hand,
These kooky adventures, I happily planned.

Through each silly mishap and comic refrain,
I dance with the mishaps, delight in the pain.
So here's to the quirks that life throws my way,
With laughter as armor, I'm ready to play!

Haphazard Harmony

I joined a new gym, thought that I'd fit,
But ended up tangled in a yoga split.
The instructor just chuckled, I joined in his glee,
Why stretch for the heavens when I can't find my knee?

A smoothie I ordered, went wild in a blaze,
It exploded like fireworks, now green on my face.
Everyone stared with a look of pure shock,
Guess I never learned how to handle a block.

Oh, the lycra I sported, such bold stripes of fate,
Made me feel like a rainbow, but twitchy and late.
I wobbled and fumbled, a blur in the room,
In this haphazard dance, I've found my own tune.

I laugh at the chaos, oh life, you're a jest,
In this bewildering journey, I'm truly obsessed.
While some take it serious, I choose to make fun,
With haphazard moves, I dance 'til I'm done.

The Fool's Guide to Living

Step one: wear your socks just a little askew,
Let them dance in the shoes, oh, what a view!
Step two: spill your drink on your brand-new shirt,
It's not just a stain; it's a badge of your hurt!

Step three: talk to the pigeons, they know how to strut,
Their wisdom is stronger than folks in a rut.
Step four: take a picture of every mishap,
Each slip and each stammer, a star on your map!

Step five: tell a joke, even if it's a flop,
The laughter that follows, oh, it never will stop.
Step six: be a fool, let the world see you shine,
In this quirky existence, your heart's the design.

With giggles and chaos, this guide I bestow,
Life's just a circus, so let your heart show!
In folly and laughter, we rise and we dive,
In this fool's guide to living, we truly arrive.

A Mischievous Twist of Fate

Fell into a puddle, oh what a sight,
Tried to walk gracefully, but gave them a fright.
A sandwich on my shirt, how did it land?
Life's little moments, all terribly planned.

Woke up late and spilled my tea,
Chasing my cat, who thought it was free.
Stepped on a toy, and then I would slip,
All in the name of a leisurely trip.

Clumsy Steps to Wisdom

Stumbled through lessons, face to the ground,
Tripped over wisdom that fell all around.
The universe chuckled, with each funny fall,
Taught me to laugh, to rise after all.

Each blunder a chapter, each mishap a page,
In the book of my journey, I take center stage.
Juggling my plans, like a clown with a flair,
Learning that wisdom comes when I dare.

The Script of Serendipity

Scripts written poorly, with typos galore,
Dramas unfolding, left me wanting more.
The banana peel tragedy, oh what a scene,
As I pirouetted, so silly and keen.

Unexpected guests at the door with surprise,
Wearing mismatched socks, what a laugh in disguise.
Coffee spilled over my favorite book,
Yet joy is found in the cracks, if you look.

Satirical Serenades

Singing my tune with a humorous twist,
Life's punchlines hidden, they persist.
With every misstep, a melody grows,
A chorus of laughter, as chaos bestows.

Dodging the awkward like a dance in the night,
Miscalculating steps, yet feeling so right.
Comedic refrains make the heart light and free,
In the madness of life, I choose comedy.

Juggling Chaos and Clarity

In a town where time runs slow,
I tripped on shoes, forgot my dough.
The juggler's act, a clumsy dance,
With oranges flying, I took a chance.

A cat in pants, a dog on skates,
I laugh as I recount my fates.
Socks unmatched, and ties askew,
Oh, the sights my days construe!

Balancing joy with a twist of fate,
I greet each gaffe, it's never late.
Every blunder, a tale to tell,
In chaos, I find my carousel.

So here's to life, a silly game,
With every error, a laugh to claim.
At the end of the day, we all will see,
Life's funny quirks are just meant to be.

The Circus of Mistakes

Welcome one, welcome all to my grand show,
Where laughter and blunders together grow.
A clown in a wig, oh what a sight,
Falling flat while trying to take flight.

A tightrope walk without a net,
I wobble and stumble, a trivial threat.
Hats fly off and pies take flight,
In this circus, it's pure delight.

Ringmaster grins with a fishy tale,
As my rubber chicken begins to flail.
Unruly giggles from the front row,
Painted faces are all aglow.

So join the fun, don't be shy,
Embrace the madness, let out a cry.
For in every stumble and every fall,
We find the humor that unites us all.

Giggles in the Gutter

Strolling through puddles, my shoes get soaked,
I slip and slide, oh how I joked!
Rain boots forgotten, I jog without care,
Catching silly glances, feels like a dare.

A sandwich drops, all mayo awry,
I laugh so hard, I might just cry.
Witty banter with squirrels nearby,
They're the true judges as they fly by.

Sidewalk chalk with a misplayed word,
I wrote 'dove', forgot 'bird'.
Neighbors chuckle at my mistake,
In the gutter, where giggles awake.

So let's embrace each twist and turn,
For in every mishap, there's always a learn.
With each misstep, let laughter accrue,
Life's a playground, meant just for you.

Umbrellas and Unfortunate Timing

Out I went with my bright red hat,
Forgot my brolly, now look at that!
The clouds erupted, rain on parade,
As I splash through puddles, a squishy cascade.

A lady sneezes, and oh what fun,
Umbrellas go tumbling, one by one.
A flurry of fabric, chaos in bloom,
In sync with the raindrops, we all find our doom.

Hold onto your hats, don't let them fly,
In this odd storm, tuxedos comply.
With giggles exploding beneath the gray skies,
We dance in the downpour with sodden surprise.

So gather your friends, and don't be shy,
With umbrellas tossed, let's wave goodbye.
For every mishap, we'll meet with a cheer,
Life's little quirks will forever endear.

Revelry in Reversals.

I tripped on my shoelace, the ground came to greet,
A dance of embarrassment, it couldn't be beat.
The world spun around, as I fell with a grin,
In this slapstick routine, who knew I'd win?

Coffee spilled on my shirt, a fashion debut,
I laughed at the chaos, life's own curfew.
Like juggling with eggs, my plans flew away,
Yet joy in the blunders brightens my day.

Every wrong turn, a new twist in the tale,
Like a merry-go-round, I'm destined to fail.
But with every misstep, my spirit prevails,
As laughter erupts like a ship with full sails.

So bring on the fumbles, the slips and the slides,
For inside these mishaps, hilarity hides.
With each twist of fate, I'll dance through the fray,
In this revelry of reversals, I find my own way.

The Clown Shoes I Wear.

With oversized shoes, I stumble and sway,
Each step's a performance, come watch me play!
A honk of a horn, my antics unfold,
In this circus of life, I'm fearless and bold.

A pie in the face, it's a classic for sure,
I laugh at the mayhem, my heart feeling pure.
Balancing snacks on my nose, such a treat,
It's sheer comic genius, a hilarious feat.

Juggling my worries, they fly in the air,
As I trip on my thoughts, but I don't really care.
Each slip on the floor brings a chuckle or two,
Life's a joke that I find, how about you?

These clown shoes I wear, they're not quite my size,
But they fit my wild spirit, so don't be surprised.
In laughter and joy, I find my true flair,
With every misstep, I declare, I'm aware!

Missteps in Merriment.

In a world of mishaps, I prance with glee,
Each blunder a marker of life's strange decree.
Tripped on a banana and danced on my way,
In this circus I call home, it's a bright cabaret.

A wrong turn taken, led to a surprise,
Met a llama in shoes, oh, how time flies!
Misjudged the jump, but who needs finesse?
With laughter and joy, I cocoon my stress.

Each tumble and fall, like laughter's sweet song,
The rhythm of errors helps me get along.
A sprinkle of chaos, a dollop of fun,
In this grand tapestry, we're all number one.

So here's to the flops and the stumbles we share,
For joy in the goof-ups is beyond compare.
Join in the missteps, let merriment ring,
In this dance of the awkward, we're all kings.

Laughter Between the Blunders.

I fumbled my way through a comedic maze,
With giggles and snickers, I navigate the craze.
A slip on the rug, as I turned with a grin,
These blunders of mine make me feel I can win.

Stumbled through stories, like stepping on ducks,
Every word's a puzzle, yet I'm out of luck.
Yet laughter's the glue that holds it all tight,
In the chaos, I find joy in the light.

A wardrobe malfunction, oh what a delight,
I wear mismatched socks, a colorful sight.
With laughter I toss all my troubles away,
In this dance of the foolish, I'll revel and play.

So bring on the errors, let the giggles abound,
For laughter between blunders is the best we have found.
With each twist of fate, I'll embrace every fall,
In this grand comedy, I'm having a ball.

www.ingramcontent.com/pod-product-compliance
Lightning Source LLC
Chambersburg PA
CBHW051644160426
43209CB00004B/784